Hinduism for E
An Introductio
Uninitiateu

Contents

Hindu Art and Culture..70

Hinduism and other religions...77

Hinduism Today 81

Conclusion..87

Introduction

Origins and History of Hinduism

Hinduism is one of the oldest religions in the world, having evolved over time within Indian society and culture. Its origins date back more than 4,000 years, although its roots are difficult to determine with certainty. Hinduism is often regarded as a fusion of spiritual and religious traditions that developed in the Indian subcontinent.

It is important to note that Hinduism was not founded by a single prophet or spiritual leader, but rather evolved over time through a complex process of cultural, religious, and philosophical interactions. The early forms of Hinduism were based on the beliefs of nomadic peoples who lived in the plains of northern India, as well as agricultural cultures that developed in the region.

Over the centuries, Hinduism transformed and adapted to social, political, and cultural changes in India. Foreign influences such as Islam and Buddhism also contributed to the transformation of Hinduism.

Hinduism has experienced several significant periods in its history. One of the oldest periods is that of the Vedas, which are considered the oldest sacred texts of Hinduism. The Vedas consist of chants and poems that were orally transmitted for centuries before being written down.

The period of the Upanishads is also considered an important period in the history of Hinduism. The Upanishads are a collection of philosophical texts that were written towards the end of the Vedic period. They present a more philosophical and spiritual vision of Hinduism, focusing on the liberation of the soul and the realization of the Self.

The medieval period in India saw the rise of different religious movements, such as Shaivism and Vaishnavism. These movements developed distinct rituals and religious practices, while maintaining the fundamental beliefs of Hinduism.

During the modern period, Hinduism faced challenges such as colonization and Westernization. However, it also witnessed the emergence of important spiritual figures like Ramakrishna and Swami Vivekananda, who worked towards the reform and revival of Hinduism.

Today, Hinduism is practiced throughout India, as well as in other parts of the world. It is known for its rich philosophical tradition, spiritual practices, and complex beliefs. Hinduism has had a significant influence on Indian culture and has also influenced many aspects of culture and spirituality worldwide.

Geographical Distribution and Demographics

The geographical distribution of Hinduism is very diverse, and there is no country with a majority Hindu population. However, India is the birthplace of Hinduism and is home to the largest Hindu population in the world, with approximately 80% of the population identifying as Hindu.

Outside of India, there are significant Hindu communities in other Asian countries such as Nepal, Sri Lanka, Bangladesh, Pakistan, Indonesia, and Malaysia. It is also estimated that there are around 1.5 million Hindu people in the United States, as well as approximately 500,000 in the United Kingdom.

In terms of demographics, Hinduism is the world's third-largest religion after Christianity and Islam, with approximately 1.2 billion followers worldwide. The Hindu population is currently growing faster than the Muslim population and is expected to surpass the number of Muslims by 2050.

However, despite this strong presence, Hindus have often faced discrimination and persecution, particularly in majority Muslim countries such as Pakistan and Bangladesh. The situation of Dalits (untouchables) in India is also a concern, as they often face discrimination based on their caste.

In summary, Hinduism is a religion with a strong presence in India, but also significant presence in other parts of Asia and around the world. While the religion has a large following, it often faces challenges and discrimination that continue to be the subject of attention and further examination.

The Main Deities

In Hinduism, deities play a central role and are worshipped in many forms and manifestations. It is important to understand that for Hindus, gods and goddesses are not seen as separate beings from the universe, but rather as emanations of the supreme divinity, Brahman.

One of the most revered deities is Vishnu, considered the protector and preserver of the universe. He is often depicted with four arms and holding symbolic objects such as a conch and a discus. Among the most well-known avatars of Vishnu are Rama, the hero of the Ramayana, and Krishna, the deity of the Bhagavad-Gita.

Shiva is another important deity in Hinduism, often associated with renewal and destruction. He is depicted with a third eye on his forehead and blue skin. Sometimes, he is depicted dancing with a snake around his neck.

The mother goddess, known as Shakti or Devi, is worshipped in many forms. She is often depicted as the driving force of the universe, the source of all energy. The goddesses Kali and Durga are two of the most well-known manifestations of the mother goddess.

Ganesh is often depicted as an elephant and is considered the god of wisdom, intelligence, and obstacle removal. He is often invoked before starting a new project or venture.

Lastly, there is Surya, the god of the sun, who is often depicted with a radiant crown and a chariot pulled by horses. He is considered the source of all life on Earth and is often invoked for health and prosperity.

Importance and Influence of Hinduism in the World

Hinduism is the third most practiced religion in the world, with approximately 1.2 billion followers. Although the majority of Hindus live in India, this religion has significant global influence. Hinduism has played a significant role in shaping Indian culture, which has in turn influenced the cultures of many other countries.

The influence of Hinduism in the world can be seen in different areas such as philosophy, literature, arts, music, cuisine, traditional medicine, ecology, and sciences. The sacred texts of Hinduism, such as the Upanishads, Bhagavad-Gita, and Puranas, have been translated into many languages and have inspired thinkers, writers, and artists worldwide.

Hinduism has also had a significant impact on Western spirituality and philosophy. Concepts of karma, reincarnation, and liberation have been adopted by many Western spiritual and religious movements. The teachings of Hinduism have also influenced Western philosophers such as Ralph Waldo Emerson and Henry David Thoreau.

Furthermore, Hinduism has a great influence on the practice of yoga and meditation worldwide. Yoga has become a popular practice in many Western countries and is often used as a means of relaxation, fitness, and spiritual development.

In the field of traditional medicine, Ayurveda, a form of ancient Indian medicine, has gained popularity worldwide. Ayurveda is based on a holistic approach to health, taking into account the whole body, mind, and soul.

Finally, Hinduism has also had an impact on environmental preservation movements. The concept of ahimsa, or non-violence, is a fundamental principle of Hinduism, which has inspired movements for animal protection, nature conservation, and sustainable development.

The Sacred Texts of Hinduism

The Vedas

The Vedas are considered the oldest and most sacred texts of Hinduism. They were transmitted orally from generation to generation for centuries before being written down in Sanskrit around 1500 BC.

The Vedas are composed of four main parts: the Rig-Veda, the Yajur-Veda, the Sama-Veda, and the Atharva-Veda. Each of these texts has its own function and importance in the practice of Hinduism.

The Rig-Veda is considered the oldest and most important of the Vedas. It contains over 1,000 hymns dedicated to various Hindu deities. Each hymn is written in Sanskrit and composed of several verses. The hymns are used during rituals and religious ceremonies.

The Yajur-Veda consists mainly of rituals and prayers to be recited during sacrifices. It is used to guide priests in performing religious ceremonies and rituals.

The Sama-Veda consists of sacred chants used during religious ceremonies. The chants are based on hymns from the Rig-Veda but are sung in a different manner.

The Atharva-Veda is considered the most recent of the Vedas and contains prayers and incantations for healing, prosperity, and protection against malevolent forces.

The Vedas have been considered the source of divine knowledge and have been used to guide the religious practices and beliefs of Hinduism. They have also influenced the culture and literature of India.

However, it is important to note that the Vedas were transmitted orally for centuries before being written down. Therefore, it is possible that certain parts may have been lost or altered over time. Additionally, the interpretation of the Vedas may vary depending on the region and Hindu school of thought.

Despite these limitations, the Vedas remain an essential part of Hindu religion and culture, offering a glimpse into the religious practice and daily life of ancient Hindus.

The Upanishads

The Upanishads are one of the most important sacred texts of Hinduism. These texts, composed between the 8th and 2nd centuries BCE, represent the wisdom of ancient sages in India. They are often considered the pinnacle of Hindu thought and have influenced many religious, philosophical, and cultural traditions in India and around the world.

The Upanishads aim to reveal the mysteries of existence and answer the big questions of life: Who are we? Where do we come from? Where are we going? They teach that the ultimate reality is Brahman, the universal divine essence that manifests in all forms of life. They also teach that the individual soul, known as Atman, is identical to Brahman and that liberation (moksha) is achieved when this unity is realized.

The Upanishads have great philosophical significance as they have influenced most schools of thought in Hinduism, including Vedanta, which is one of the most popular schools today. They have also influenced other spiritual traditions such as Buddhism, Jainism, and Sikhism.

The Upanishads also teach key concepts such as karma, reincarnation, and dharma. Karma is the law of cause and effect that governs the cycle of birth and death. Reincarnation is the belief that the soul survives after death and is reborn in another form of life. Dharma is the moral and ethical duty of every individual that must be followed to live a fulfilled life in harmony with society and the universe.

The Upanishads are also rich in symbols and metaphors that illustrate complex philosophical concepts. For example, the famous metaphor of the mustard seed explains that the ultimate reality is both infinitely small and infinitely great, just like the mustard seed that is both very small yet can become a large plant.

The Mahabharata and the Bhagavad-Gita

The Mahabharata is one of the oldest and most important texts of Hinduism, and it is considered a fundamental source of Hindu tradition. It is an epic that tells the story of the

Bharata dynasty and consists of 18 books and over 100,000 verses. The Bhagavad-Gita is a part of the Mahabharata that was written between the 5th and 2nd centuries BCE. It is considered one of the most important texts of Hinduism and has had a significant influence on Indian culture and thought.

The Bhagavad-Gita is a conversation between the prince Arjuna and the god Krishna. Arjuna is about to go into war against his own people, but he is hesitant because he realizes that it means killing members of his own family. Krishna, who is the incarnation of God, explains to him that the war is just and that he must fulfill his duty to his kingdom and family. The Bhagavad-Gita is a deeply philosophical text that explores themes such as duty, karma, reincarnation, and self-realization.

The Mahabharata is an epic story that narrates the rivalry between the two branches of the Bharata dynasty. The Pandavas, who are the heroes of the story, are the sons of Pandu, while the Kauravas are the sons of Dhritarashtra. The rivalry between the two branches leads to a great war, the battle of Kurukshetra, which is described in detail in the book of the Bhagavad-Gita. The Mahabharata is a complex story that explores many themes, including honor, loyalty, family, justice, and morality.

The Mahabharata and the Bhagavad-Gita have had a significant influence on Indian culture and thought. They have been studied and commented upon for centuries, and they continue to be a source of inspiration for Hindus worldwide. The teachings of the Bhagavad-Gita have been used to justify social and political movements, including the Indian independence movement led by Mahatma Gandhi.

The Ramayana

The Ramayana is one of the most important texts of Hinduism and one of the most popular worldwide. It tells the epic story of Rama, a prince who embodies virtue and justice, and his wife Sita, who is abducted by the demon Ravana. The Ramayana is a story full of adventures, twists, and memorable characters, but it also teaches important values for Hindus.

The Ramayana is composed of seven books, called kandas, which tell the story of Rama from his birth to his triumphant return to Ayodhya. The kandas are as follows:

Balakanda: The book of childhood, which tells the birth of Rama and his education.

Ayodhyakanda: The book of exile, which narrates the exile of Rama and his wife Sita in the forest for fourteen years.

Aranyakanda: The book of the forest, which tells their life in the forest and the abduction of Sita by Ravana.

Kishkindhakanda: The book of Kishkindha, which narrates Rama's alliance with the monkeys to free Sita.

Sundarakanda: The book of beauty, which tells the efforts of Hanuman to find Sita.

Yuddhakanda: The book of war, which describes the final battle between Rama and Ravana.

Uttarakanda: The final book, which narrates Rama's return to Ayodhya and his life as a king.

The Ramayana is an important text for Hindus as it teaches values such as loyalty, honor, justice, and compassion. It also shows the triumph of good over evil and how people from all social classes can achieve liberation (moksha) by following the path of virtue.

The Ramayana is also a source of inspiration for Indian art and culture. Depictions of Rama, Sita, Hanuman, and other characters from the Ramayana can be found in art, literature, dance, and music. The stories of the Ramayana are told in puppet shows, films, television series, and video games.

The Puranas

The Puranas are a collection of sacred Hindu texts that contain stories, myths, laws, and rituals. They were written between 400 and 1000 AD and are considered the second category of sacred Hindu texts, after the Vedas. The Puranas are written in Sanskrit but have been translated into many languages worldwide.

The Puranas contain narratives about major Hindu deities such as Vishnu, Shiva, Brahma, Durga, Ganesha, and many others. They also explain key concepts of Hinduism, such as karma, reincarnation, and liberation (moksha). The Puranas are therefore an important source for understanding Hindu mythology and the fundamental beliefs of this religion.

In addition to stories and myths, the Puranas also contain information on Hindu practices and rituals. For example, they explain how to perform pujas (offerings) to honor the deities, how to celebrate festivals and religious ceremonies, and how to live an ethical life according to the principles of Hinduism.

The Puranas are divided into 18 main texts, each dedicated to a particular deity or specific theme. The most well-known are the Vishnu Purana, the Shiva Purana, the Bhagavata Purana, and the Markandeya Purana.

The Puranas have had a significant influence on Hindu culture and religion. They have inspired works of art, songs, dances, and plays. They have also influenced the practices and beliefs of Hinduism, providing guidance on how to lead a religious and ethical life.

The Texts of Tantra

The section on Tantra texts is an important part of understanding Hinduism. Tantra texts are sacred scriptures that focus on expanding consciousness and self-realization. They are often associated with ritual practices that include yoga, meditation, visualization, chanting of mantras, and sacred sexuality.

Tantra texts are written in Sanskrit, an ancient language of India, and cover a wide range of topics. Some texts focus on tantric practices, while others deal with philosophy, cosmology, and spirituality.

Tantra texts also include practical manuals for practitioners, providing instructions on spiritual practices. They often describe complex and detailed rituals aimed at helping the practitioner connect with their inner divine.

Tantra texts have a holistic view of life and include teachings on all aspects of existence, including sexuality, food, medicine, ecology, art, and culture. Tantra texts emphasize the importance of balance between body, mind, and soul.

Tantra texts have been widely misunderstood and misinterpreted over the years, partly due to their association with sacred sexuality. However, sacred sexuality is only a part of the teachings of Tantra and must be understood within its spiritual context.

Tantra texts are of great importance in Hinduism, but they are also studied in other spiritual traditions such as Buddhism and Jainism. Tantra texts have had a significant influence on the art, culture, and spirituality of India, as well as on the development of traditional Indian medicine (Ayurveda)..

Philosophical Foundations

The Six Schools of Thought (Darshanas)

The six schools of thought (Darshanas) of Hinduism represent different philosophical perspectives on the universe and the nature of reality. Each school offers its own unique vision of existence, but all seek to understand the ultimate reality. In this section, we will explore the six schools of thought in Hinduism in detail.

Samkhya: The Samkhya school, founded by the sage Kapila, considers the universe to be composed of two fundamental entities: matter (prakriti) and spirit (purusha). According to this school, the liberation of the soul occurs when one understands the nature of these two entities and separates them.

Yoga: The Yoga school, whose founder is Patanjali, focuses on the practice of meditation and asceticism to achieve liberation of the soul. This school teaches the importance of controlling the mind and body to achieve the state of Samadhi, where one attains union with the Absolute.

Nyaya: The Nyaya school, founded by Gautama, is a school of logic and reasoning. This school emphasizes the importance of argumentation and proof to attain ultimate truth. According to this school, the liberation of the soul is achieved by understanding the nature of reality through logic and reasoning.

Vaisheshika: The Vaisheshika school, founded by Kanada, is a metaphysical school that focuses on the analysis of physical reality and its constituents. This school considers the ultimate reality to be composed of tiny atoms (anu), and the liberation of the soul is attained by understanding the nature of these atoms.

Mimamsa: The Mimamsa school, founded by Jaimini, focuses on the study of sacred texts (Vedas) and religious rituals. This school believes that the liberation of the soul is achieved by performing the religious rituals prescribed by the Vedas.

Vedanta: The Vedanta school, whose most famous representatives are Shankara, Ramanuja, and Madhva, focuses on the study of sacred texts (Upanishads) and the identification of the ultimate nature of existence. This school teaches that the ultimate reality is the Absolute (Brahman), which is the only true reality, and that each individual soul (Atman) is a manifestation of this Absolute. The liberation of the soul is achieved by realizing this union with the Absolute.

Each school of thought offers its own perspective on ultimate reality and the liberation of the soul. By studying the different schools of thought, one can discover the immense richness and depth of Hindu philosophy.

Debates and Dialogues

Debates and dialogues are fundamental elements of Hinduism, which has always encouraged the search for truth through discussion and reflection. This approach has led to the emergence of different schools of thought, each with its own vision of ultimate reality. Debates and dialogues have enabled Hindu thinkers to develop innovative theories and concepts, as well as to clarify the ambiguities and contradictions of sacred texts.

One of the main debates in Hinduism concerns the nature of ultimate reality, which Hindus call Brahman. According to different schools of thought, Brahman is either a personal entity, an impersonal entity, or both. Schools of thought that consider Brahman as a personal entity often describe it as a supreme deity, while those that consider it as an impersonal entity often describe it as a universal cosmic energy.

Another important debate concerns the relationship between Brahman and the individual soul, called Atman. Some schools of thought believe that the individual soul is identical to Brahman, while others maintain that it is distinct from Brahman but can be united with it through meditation and spiritual practice.

Another subject of debate is the nature of karma and its impact on human life. Some schools of thought believe that karma is deterministic, meaning that past actions determine the individual's fate, while others argue that the individual's free will can influence karma and thus change their destiny.

Debates and dialogues have also focused on the practices and rituals of Hinduism, including the importance of vegetarianism, ahimsa (non-violence), yoga, and meditation. Debates have also addressed the question of whether these practices are necessary for attaining spiritual liberation or if they simply serve as means to enhance the quality of life.

Finally, debates and dialogues have touched upon the question of whether Hinduism is a religion or a philosophy. Some Hindu thinkers consider Hinduism primarily as a way of life philosophy, while others argue that it is a complete religion with its own practices and rituals.

The Synthesis of Philosophy and Religion

The synthesis of philosophy and religion is at the heart of Hinduism. Hinduism is a complex religion characterized by its diversity of philosophical and religious traditions. This religion emerged from the fusion of various schools of thought, beliefs, and religious practices. This unique synthesis of philosophy and religion is evident in many aspects of Hindus' daily lives.

The philosophy of Hinduism is based on the six schools of thought (Darshanas) that have developed complex and sophisticated systems of thought. These schools focus on understanding reality, the essence of existence, and the relationship between man and the divine. They have developed a comprehensive and unified vision of the universe that integrates philosophy, metaphysics, ethics, and spirituality.

The religion of Hinduism, on the other hand, is based on beliefs and practices aimed at realizing the union of the individual soul with the divine. The concepts of Dharma, Karma, Samsara, and Moksha are key elements of Hindu religion. The religion of Hinduism is based on the belief that the existence of each individual is governed by the cycle of life and death. The ultimate goal of the religion is to enable each individual soul to break free from the cycle of reincarnation and realize union with the divine.

Hence, Hinduism is a unique synthesis of philosophy and religion. This synthesis is evident in many aspects of Hindus' daily lives, such as religious rituals, yoga and meditation practices, food and dietary habits, social relationships, music, and art. This synthesis has also led to numerous philosophical debates and dialogues within the Hindu community.

Ultimately, the synthesis of philosophy and religion in Hinduism enables Hindus to develop a comprehensive and unified understanding of the universe. This synthesis provides Hindus with a profound and coherent vision of reality and their place in the world. It also allows Hindus to live their lives in a harmonious and balanced way, balancing their intellectual and spiritual development. In summary, the synthesis of philosophy and religion is one of the most important and fascinating aspects of Hinduism, and it deserves to be studied in depth to better understand this complex and fascinating religion.

Beliefs and Key Concepts

Dharma

Dharma is one of the most important concepts in Hinduism. It is difficult to translate literally, but can be understood as a set of divine laws, duties, and responsibilities that govern the universe and the life of every human being. Dharma is closely related to the concepts of karma, reincarnation, and liberation, and is often described as the path of virtue and righteousness.

Dharma can be divided into several categories, each with its own significance. Firstly, there is the universal dharma, which applies to all living beings in the universe and involves maintaining balance and harmony in creation. Then there is social dharma, which refers to the duties and obligations of each individual towards their family, community, and society. This social dharma is closely linked to castes, social classes, and professions, and aims to maintain order and stability in society. Lastly, there is personal dharma, which refers to the duties and responsibilities of each individual towards themselves as spiritual beings seeking liberation.

Dharma is a complex and often misunderstood concept, as it can be interpreted in different ways depending on social and cultural contexts. However, a clear understanding of dharma is essential to grasp the essence of Hinduism and its significance for believers.

To better understand the concept of dharma, it can be helpful to use an analogy. Dharma is often compared to the law of gravity. Just as gravity maintains order and balance in the universe, dharma maintains order and balance in creation. Just as gravity affects all objects in the universe, dharma applies to all living beings in the universe. Just as gravity is invisible but omnipresent, dharma is often invisible but omnipresent in the life of every individual.

Karma

Karma is a central concept in Hinduism and is often misunderstood by non-initiates. In simple terms, karma refers to the law of cause and effect. In other words, every action we perform, whether good or bad, has consequences that impact our present and future lives. This notion of retribution is intimately connected to the idea of reincarnation, as the consequences of our actions in this life determine the nature of our next life.

Karma is a concept that exists in many cultures and religions, but in Hinduism, it is particularly complex and developed. According to sacred texts, there are three types of karma: Sanchita karma, Prarabdha karma, and Kriyamana karma. Sanchita karma is the accumulated karma from all our past lives, Prarabdha karma is the karma that is active in this current life, and Kriyamana karma is the karma we create in every moment through our present actions.

The ultimate goal of life in Hinduism is to break free from the cycle of reincarnation, to end suffering, and to realize unity with the divine. To achieve this state of liberation, it is necessary to work on one's karma. In other words, one must strive to perform positive actions and avoid negative actions in order to minimize the negative impact of karma on one's current and future lives.

The idea of karma is often misconstrued in the West, where it is often equated with some sort of law of the jungle or divine judgment. However, Hinduism does not see karma as a system of punishment or reward, but rather as a natural process of cause and effect. Furthermore, it is important to emphasize that karma is not intended to discourage people from doing good, but rather to encourage them to act responsibly and take accountability for their actions.

Samsara and Reincarnation

The belief in reincarnation is at the core of Hinduism. According to this belief, every human being is an eternal being or «atman,» destined to be reincarnated after death. The process of reincarnation is called «samsara» and is considered an endless cycle of birth, death, and rebirth.

The theory of reincarnation is based on the principle of karma, which is a universal law that states every action has consequences. According to this law, every action, thought, or word is recorded and evaluated for the purpose of rewards or punishments, which will determine the quality of the next life.

The quality of the next life also depends on the actions, thoughts, and words of the current life. Therefore, the ultimate goal of each individual is to purify their soul or «karma» to achieve liberation, known as «moksha.»

The concept of samsara and reincarnation is closely connected to the four goals of life, or the «Purusharthas.» The Purusharthas include material prosperity, sexual satisfaction, pursuit of knowledge, and spiritual liberation. According to Hinduism, each individual must achieve these goals to attain moksha, which is the ultimate liberation from samsara.

The belief in reincarnation has a significant impact on the daily life of Hindus. It influences their attitude towards death and the afterlife, as well as their behavior towards other living beings. Hindus view life as sacred and believe it is important to treat all living beings with compassion and respect.

Moksha (Liberation)

Moksha, or liberation, is a central concept in Hinduism. According to this religion, every human being is bound to the cycle of life and death, known as samsara, due to their past actions, karma. The ultimate goal of Hinduism is to break free from this cycle of reincarnation and attain moksha, which is the state of liberation of the soul.

Moksha is the realization of the purpose of human existence, and it is a state of eternal bliss, peace, and happiness. It is described as a freedom from pain, suffering, and ignorance, and a merging of the individual soul with the universal soul, Brahman. In this state, the individual soul is liberated from all limitations of consciousness and ego and becomes one with the universal soul.

There are several methods to attain moksha, each based on different spiritual practices. The path of knowledge, Jnana Yoga, is one of the most common ways to attain moksha. This path involves the knowledge of the soul and Brahman through contemplation, meditation, and the study of sacred texts.

Bhakti Yoga, or the path of devotion, is another way to attain moksha. This practice involves intense devotion to a particular Hindu deity and unconditional love for that deity.

Karma Yoga, the path of selfless action, is another method of attaining moksha. This practice involves performing selfless acts for the love of humanity, without any attachment to the fruits of the action.

Lastly, Raja Yoga, or the path of meditation, is another practice to attain moksha. This path involves strict discipline of body and mind through meditation, breath control, and concentration.

It is important to note that moksha is a concept that goes beyond religion, as it transcends the boundaries of religion and culture. It is a state of consciousness that can be achieved by anyone who aspires to the liberation of the soul.

Brahman and Atman

In Hinduism, Brahman and Atman are two central concepts that form the basis of Hindu philosophy and spirituality. According to Hindu tradition, Brahman is the supreme essence of the universe, the ultimate and universal reality, while Atman is the individual essence, the soul or the self.

Brahman is considered the source of all creation and the driving force that keeps the universe in motion. It is the eternal and unchanging essence that lies behind all forms of reality. According to Hindu sacred texts, Brahman is often described as formless, attributeless, and indescribable. Brahman is present in everything that exists, from the smallest subatomic particle to the largest galaxy.

On the other hand, Atman is the individual essence of every living being. According to Hindu philosophy, Atman is identical to Brahman, meaning that every individual possesses a spark of the same divine essence as that of the universe. Atman is considered immortal and eternal, and it is the source of consciousness, intelligence, and individual identity.

Understanding the relationship between Brahman and Atman is essential to Hindu spirituality. The ultimate goal of Hindu spiritual practice is to realize the union between the individual Atman and the universal Brahman, often referred to as moksha or liberation. This union is achieved through the practice of yoga, meditation, and other spiritual practices.

It is important to note that the understanding of Brahman and Atman can vary among different schools of Hindu thought, and there are many different interpretations of these concepts. However, the idea of the unity between the individual and the universe remains at the core of Hindu spirituality.

The Four Goals of Life (Purusharthas)

The Purusharthas, also known as the «Four Goals of Life,» are a central concept in Hinduism. These four goals are considered the ultimate purposes of human existence, and each individual must pursue them in order to achieve a fulfilled and meaningful life.

The first goal is dharma, which is generally translated as «duty» or «law.» Dharma refers to the duties and obligations that every individual must fulfill in order to maintain order and harmony in society. This includes responsibilities towards family, community, environment, and society as a whole. Dharma is regarded as the foundation for all other goals of life.

The second goal is artha, which is translated as «wealth» or «success.» Artha refers to the pursuit of material and financial prosperity, but not at the expense of dharma. The goal of artha is to enable an individual to fulfill their duties and obligations towards society.

The third goal is kama, which is translated as «pleasure» or «desire.» Kama refers to the fulfillment of desires and sensual pleasures, such as love, romance, and sexuality. However, these pleasures should not be pursued excessively or at the expense of other goals of life.

The fourth and final goal is moksha, which is translated as «liberation» or «salvation.» Moksha refers to the liberation of the soul from the endless cycle of birth, death, and reincarnation. It is the ultimate goal of human existence and can be attained through the practice of yoga, meditation, and self-realization.

It is important to note that the Purusharthas are not separate goals, but rather complementary aspects of life. Each goal must be pursued in a balanced manner and in harmony with the others in order to achieve a fulfilled life.

Furthermore, the importance given to each goal may vary depending on individuals and stages of their life. For example, a young adult may be more focused on artha and kama, while an older individual may place greater emphasis on dharma and moksha.

In summary, the Purusharthas provide a philosophical framework for a fulfilled and accomplished life. They encourage balance and harmony between different facets of life, while offering the opportunity to attain ultimate spiritual liberation.

The Four Eras of the World (Yugas)

The four eras of the world, also known as the Yugas, are an important doctrine in Hinduism that explains how the world evolves through cycles. According to this doctrine, time is cyclical and consists of four ages, each subsequent age being shorter and less perfect than the previous one.

The first age is called Satya Yuga, or the Age of Truth. It is an age of perfection, purity, and truth, where human beings are highly spiritual and have a harmonious relationship with nature. The duration of this age is 1,728,000 divine years.

The second age is called Treta Yuga, or the Silver Age. In this age, human beings are less spiritual than in Satya Yuga, but they are still close to perfection. The duration of this age is 1,296,000 divine years.

The third age is called Dvapara Yuga, or the Bronze Age. In this age, spirituality decreases significantly, and human beings become increasingly focused on material desires. The duration of this age is 864,000 divine years.

Finally, the fourth and last age is called Kali Yuga, or the Iron Age. It is the shortest and least perfect age of all, where spirituality is at its lowest and human beings are most focused on material desires. The duration of this age is 432,000 divine years.

According to the doctrine of the Yugas, the world goes through these cyclical periods uninterrupted, and we are currently in the period of Kali Yuga. However, it is important to note that Hinduism also teaches that each age is followed by a transitional period, called Sandhi, which lasts 10% of the duration of the respective age. This transitional period allows human beings to prepare for the transition to the new age.

The Yugas thus present a cyclical view of the history of the world, where each age represents a stage in the evolution of humanity. This doctrine provides an important source of reflection for Hindus, as they seek to understand their place in the world and their relationship with nature and the universe.

Practices and Rituals

Rites of Passage (Samskaras)

Rites of passage, or samskaras, are significant ceremonies in the life of a Hindu. They mark key stages of life, from birth to death, including initiation into the study of sacred texts and marriage. Samskaras help purify and bless the body and soul, and are considered essential for a successful life.

The first of the samskaras is the birth ceremony, or Jatakarma. This ceremony is celebrated shortly after the birth of a child and involves a blessing for the newborn and the mother. The second samskara is the naming ceremony, or Namakarana. This takes place 12 days after birth and involves giving a name to the baby.

The third samskara is the initiation into study, or Upanayana. This ceremony marks the beginning of learning sacred texts and is reserved for boys. It takes place between 8 and 12 years of age and involves a purification and blessing ceremony for the boy, who is then initiated into the study of sacred texts.

Marriage, or Vivaha, is considered the fourth samskara. It is one of the most important and elaborate samskaras, marking the union of two individuals for life. The marriage ceremony is rich in symbols and rituals, accompanied by chants and prayers.

The fifth samskara is the funeral ceremony, or Antyesti. This ceremony takes place after the death of a person and marks their departure to the afterlife. The ashes of the deceased are typically scattered in a sacred river, such as the Ganges.

In addition to these five main samskaras, there are many others that mark important stages of life, such as the ceremony of the first solid food, or Annaprashana, or the ceremony of the first haircut, or Chudakarana.

Pujas and Offerings

The practice of pujas and offerings is an integral part of Hinduism, and is considered a form of communication with the deities. Pujas are rituals that involve offerings of flowers, food, lamps, and incense to the gods and goddesses, accompanied by prayers and chants. Offerings are meticulously prepared to honor the deities and show them respect and gratitude.

Pujas can be performed at home, in temples, or during festivals and important ceremonies. Each deity has their own specific rituals and offerings, and believers choose the ones that best suit their relationship with the particular deity. For example, an offering of milk and fruits is common for the goddess Ganga, while an offering of honey and milk is often associated with the god Krishna.

The practice of pujas is often accompanied by the recitation of mantras, devotional chants, and the reading of sacred texts. These elements are considered essential for establishing a deep connection with the deities and receiving their blessings. Music also plays an important role in pujas, with many instruments like tambourines, harmoniums, and tablas being used to accompany the chants.

Offerings play a significant role in pujas, as they symbolize the believers' respect and gratitude towards the deities. Offerings can consist of food, drinks, flowers, incense, and lamps, as well as jewelry and precious objects. Offerings are typically placed on an altar or shrine and presented to the deities during the puja ritual.

Pujas and offerings are highly important practices in Hinduism, as they enable believers to connect with the deities and receive their blessings. These rituals are considered expressions of devotion and gratitude and are an integral part of Hindus' daily lives. Pujas and offerings also showcase the richness and diversity of Hinduism, as they vary according to the deities, regions, and local traditions.

Festivals and Celebrations

Festivals and celebrations are significant aspects of Hindu culture. Hindus celebrate numerous festivals throughout the year, with some being celebrated nationwide and others specific to a region or community.

Festivals are often associated with mythological and religious events and provide an opportunity for Hindus to connect with their beliefs and culture. Additionally, festivals offer a chance to strengthen family and community bonds.

The most important festival in Hinduism is Diwali, also known as the «Festival of Lights.» This festival is celebrated in October or November and lasts for five days. Hindus light diyas (oil lamps) to symbolize the victory of light over darkness and good over evil. Fireworks illuminate the night sky while families gather to share meals and exchange gifts.

Holi is another significant festival celebrated in March. Also known as the «Festival of Colors,» it marks the end of winter and the arrival of spring. People throw colored powder at each other, spray water, and dance to celebrate life and joy.

Durga Puja is a major festival celebrated in the eastern regions of India. It is dedicated to the goddess Durga and is observed for nine days in September or October. Hindus celebrate this festival by organizing pujas, singing, and dancing in honor of the goddess.

Janmashtami is a festival celebrated in August or September to mark the birth of Lord Krishna. Hindus observe this festival by performing pujas, singing, dancing, and holding processions.

Other important Hindu festivals include Navaratri, Raksha Bandhan, Ganesh Chaturthi, Onam, Pongal, and Baisakhi. All these festivals are celebrated with rituals, chants, dances, and offerings, which vary according to region and community.

Pilgrimages

Pilgrimages are an important practice in Hinduism, allowing believers to connect with deities and strengthen their faith. Hindu pilgrimage sites are often considered holy places where significant events from Hindu mythology are believed to have taken place.

The most famous Hindu pilgrimage is to Amarnath, located in the Himalayan mountains. This pilgrimage attracts thousands of devotees every year who come to worship the Hindu deity Shiva and is considered one of the most challenging in the world due to high altitude and difficult terrain.

Another significant Hindu pilgrimage site is the Kumbh Mela, which takes place every 12 years and attracts millions of pilgrims from around the world. The Kumbh Mela is a celebration of spiritual purification, where believers bathe in the sacred rivers of India to cleanse themselves of sins.

Other important pilgrimage sites in India include the Tirumala Venkateswara Temple in Tirupati, where believers come to worship the god Vishnu, and the Vaishno Devi Temple in the Himalayas, which is dedicated to the Hindu goddess Durga.

Pilgrimage is often associated with the practice of walking, which is considered an act of devotion towards the deities. Believers may walk for kilometers or even hundreds of kilometers to reach the pilgrimage site, and this practice is seen as a way to get closer to the deities and strengthen one's faith.

Yoga and Meditation

Yoga and meditation hold significant places in Hinduism. Yoga is a physical, mental, and spiritual practice aimed at achieving balance and harmony within oneself. Meditation, on the other hand, is a technique of mental concentration aiming to calm the mind and achieve inner peace.

In Hinduism, yoga is considered a sacred practice associated with spirituality and religion. It is seen as a means to get closer to God and unite with the divine essence present in each of us. Yoga is often associated with the practice of asanas, physical postures that strengthen the body and enhance flexibility. However, yoga also encompasses breathing techniques, meditation, and relaxation.

Meditation is a practice that is highly significant in Hinduism as well. It is regarded as a way to calm the mind and connect with the divine essence present in each of us. Meditation can be practiced in various ways, depending on one's goals and needs. Some meditation practices focus on breathing, while others center on visualization or repetition of mantras.

Yoga and meditation are often associated with health benefits. These practices can reduce stress, improve concentration, strengthen the immune system, and prevent certain diseases. However, it is important to note that yoga and meditation are primarily spiritual practices aimed at developing self-awareness and connecting with the divine essence present in each of us.

Vegetarianism and Ahimsa

In Hinduism, vegetarianism and ahimsa (non-violence) are important principles that greatly influence the daily lives of Hindus. Ahimsa is the practice of non-violence towards all living beings, including animals, and is considered one of the fundamental principles of Hinduism. Vegetarians believe that consuming meat goes against ahimsa, as it involves the suffering and death of a living being.

Vegetarianism is therefore regarded as a lifestyle that respects life and the environment and is widely practiced in India, especially among Hindu communities. Vegetarianism is often associated with the practice of yoga and meditation, which promote self-awareness and empathy towards other living beings.

The significance of ahimsa and vegetarianism in Hinduism can be understood through analogies with nature and animals. Hindus believe that all living beings are interconnected and part of a larger ecosystem. Therefore, ahimsa is seen as a means to maintain balance and harmony in this ecosystem by avoiding harm to other living beings and their well-being.

Moreover, ahimsa is considered a spiritual practice that can help attain liberation (moksha) from the cycle of reincarnation (samsara) and get closer to the ultimate divinity (Brahman). By refraining from causing harm to other living beings, Hindus believe that one can achieve a higher state of consciousness and greater inner peace.

However, it is important to note that vegetarianism is not universally practiced in Hinduism, and some communities and regions in India do consume meat. Furthermore, vegetarianism should not be regarded as a religious obligation but rather as a personal practice based on individual beliefs and spirituality.

Lastly, it is important to highlight that ahimsa and vegetarianism also have broader social and environmental implications. By avoiding meat consumption, Hindus can contribute to reducing the environmental impact of intensive agriculture and industrial farming. Additionally, ahimsa can be extended to social and political relationships by promoting non-violence and compassion towards all human beings, regardless of their ethnic, religious, or political backgrounds.

Branches and Schools of Hinduism

Vedicism

Vedicism is considered the earliest form of Hinduism and dates back approximately 3,500 years to the Bronze Age in India. This period was marked by the arrival of Indo-Aryan tribes in the Indus Valley, bringing with them a polytheistic religion that would later be incorporated into Hinduism. The sacred texts of Vedicism are the Vedas, which are regarded as the oldest religious texts in the world.

The Vedas are divided into four parts: the Rig Veda, Sama Veda, Yajur Veda, and Atharva Veda. The Rig Veda is the oldest and most important of these texts, consisting of over a thousand hymns to various deities, prayers, and rituals. The Vedas are written in Sanskrit, an ancient language that has influenced many others.

Vedicism was a religion centered around sacrifices, with priests (the Brahmins) acting as intermediaries between humans and gods. The sacrifices were performed to gain favor from the gods, who were believed to have the power to grant life and prosperity. Sacrifices were also conducted to purify sins and wrongdoings.

Vedicism was highly ritualistic, and the priests held a central position in society. Castes began to form during this time, with the Brahmins occupying the highest position. Vedicism also evolved into Brahmanism, a more sophisticated form of the religion focused on the study of sacred texts and meditation.

Today, Vedicism is no longer practiced as a distinct religion, but its practices and teachings have been incorporated into Hinduism. The Vedas continue to be studied and chanted during religious ceremonies, and sacrifices have been replaced by other practices such as pujas (offerings) and meditation.

Shaivism

Shaivism is one of the major branches of Hinduism, centered around devotion to the deity Shiva, regarded as the highest reality or ultimate truth. Shaivites believe in the omnipresence of Shiva, present in every aspect of existence, and seek to achieve union with him through the practice of meditation, devotion, and ascetic life.

Shaivism is present throughout India but is more widespread in the northern and western regions. It has also influenced religious traditions in Southeast Asia and the Himalayas. Devotion to Shiva dates back to prehistoric times, and temples dedicated to Shiva have existed for over two thousand years. Shaivites are known for their ascetic practices and reverence for Shiva in various forms, representing different aspects of his divine being.

Shaivism focuses on meditation, devotion, and contemplation of Shiva, with the ultimate goal of achieving liberation (moksha) from the cycle of birth and death. Shaivite practices include yoga, prayer, chanting of mantras, rituals, and offerings. Shaivism has also produced numerous sacred texts, with the most famous being the Shiva Purana and the Linga Purana.

Shaivism is often associated with destruction and transformation, but this interpretation is often misunderstood. Shiva is not merely a destructive force, but rather a force of transformation that liberates the soul from illusion and suffering. This transformation is symbolized by the cycle of life, death, and rebirth, and the most well-known symbol of Shaivism is the lingam, representing Shiva's creative power.

Shaivism is rich in art and culture and has influenced various art forms, from classical Indian dance to sculpture. Shaivites have also created many stories and legends explaining the different forms of Shiva and their significance. Shaivism has also influenced neighboring religions and cultures, including Buddhism and Jainism.

Vaishnavism

Vaishnavism is one of the most popular branches of Hinduism, with over 600 million followers worldwide. This tradition emphasizes devotion to Vishnu, one of the most important gods in Hindu mythology.

Vaishnavism is based on the belief that Vishnu is the supreme god who maintains order and balance in the universe. Vaishnavas believe that devotion to Vishnu can lead to liberation from reincarnation and union with the universal soul.

The Bhagavata Purana, an important sacred text for Vaishnavas, describes the ten avatars of Vishnu, known as the Dashavatara. Each avatar has a unique story and is considered an incarnation of Vishnu to help maintain order in the universe.

Vaishnavism is also known for its practice of bhakti yoga, a form of yoga that involves devotion and love towards God. Practitioners of bhakti yoga seek to develop a personal relationship with Vishnu through meditation, prayer, chanting of bhajans (devotional songs), and the practice of ahimsa (non-violence).

The worship of Krishna is a specific form of Vaishnavism that emphasizes devotion to Krishna, an incarnation of Vishnu. Followers of Krishna devote themselves to a spiritual life centered on devotion, meditation, and service to the community.

In the Vaishnava tradition, love and respect for all living beings are also highly important. Practitioners seek to live in harmony with the environment and preserve life in all its forms.

Shaktism

Shaktism is one of the major branches of Hinduism that focuses on the divine feminine power, known as Shakti, represented in various divine forms. This branch of Hinduism is highly influential in contemporary India and worldwide.

Shaktism is based on the belief that the supreme divinity, called Brahman, is both masculine and feminine. Shakti represents the feminine aspect of this divinity, considered as the creative energy of the universe. Shaktism followers believe that the divine feminine power is present in every living being, with each individual embodying a part of this energy.

Shakti is represented in various divine forms, such as Durga, Kali, Parvati, and Lakshmi. Each of these divine forms has its own symbolic meaning and specific attributes. For example, Durga represents strength and determination, Kali represents the destruction of negative forces, Parvati represents love and compassion, and Lakshmi represents wealth and prosperity.

Worship of Shakti often involves spiritual practices such as meditation, yoga, and offering symbolic objects like flowers, fruits, and jewelry. Rituals and celebrations associated with Shaktism are often based on the Hindu lunar calendar, with important festivals such as Navratri, which celebrates the victory of the goddess Durga over the demon Mahishasura.

Shaktism has also influenced Indian art and culture, with sculptures and paintings dedicated to the various divine forms of Shakti. Classical Indian dance, such as Bharatanatyam, is often associated with the worship of Shakti, featuring choreographies dedicated to various female deities.

Shaktism has also faced controversies, particularly regarding the role of women in the religion. Some critics have accused Shaktism of having an essentialist view of gender and limiting women's participation in religious practices.

Philosophical Schools (Darshanas)

The philosophical schools of Hinduism, also known as Darshanas, are six systems of thought that have developed over centuries in India. Though each of these schools has its own perspective and method to understand the ultimate reality, their common aim is to comprehend the nature of existence and achieve liberation.

The first system of thought is Samkhya, which considers the ultimate reality as composed of two fundamental elements: Purusha and Prakriti. Purusha represents the eternal soul, while Prakriti represents primordial matter. The purpose of life, according to Samkhya, is to attain liberation by understanding the nature of Purusha and liberating oneself from the grip of Prakriti.

The second system of thought is Yoga, which seeks to achieve the union of the individual with the divine through spiritual practices such as meditation and the practice of asanas. Yoga considers the mind as the key to understanding the ultimate reality and attaining liberation.

The third system of thought is Nyaya, which focuses on logic and knowledge. Nyaya considers knowledge as the key to liberation and logic as an indispensable tool to attain that knowledge.

The fourth system of thought is Vaisheshika, which centers around ontology and metaphysics. Vaisheshika considers the ultimate reality as composed of atoms and the knowledge of these atoms as the key to understanding the nature of existence.

The fifth system of thought is Mimamsa, which concentrates on rituals and religious practices. Mimamsa considers the study of sacred texts and the practice of rituals as the key to understanding the nature of existence and achieving liberation.

Finally, the sixth system of thought is Vedanta, which focuses on the Upanishads and the Brahma Sutras. Vedanta considers the ultimate reality as Brahman, the divine essence of the universe. The purpose of life, according to Vedanta, is to achieve union with Brahman through self-knowledge and understanding the nature of existence.

Each of these systems of thought offers a unique perspective on the ultimate reality and methods to achieve liberation. While some of these systems may be more popular than others in India, all have contributed to the richness and diversity of Hindu culture. Understanding these philosophical schools is essential to comprehending Hinduism as a whole.

Everyday Life and Hinduism

Customs and Family Traditions

In Hinduism, customs and family traditions play a central role in the lives of Hindus. The family is considered the cornerstone of Hindu society and is the basic unit of social life. Family members support and help each other in all stages of life.

One of the most important family customs is the veneration of ancestors. Hindus believe that the souls of ancestors continue to exist after their death and they can either help or harm the lives of their descendants. To honor their ancestors, Hindus offer prayers and offerings during festivals and rituals.

Dowry is another important custom in Hindu society. It consists of a gift of money, jewelry, or material possessions that the bride's family gives to the groom's family. Although this custom is practiced less frequently, it still exists in certain regions of India.

Marriage is also a significant family event in Hinduism. Marriages are often arranged by the families of both partners and are considered a sacred union that lasts a lifetime. Hindu wedding ceremonies are extremely colorful and involve complex rituals that symbolize the union of two souls.

Food is also an important element of Hindu family customs. Hindus are known for their diverse and delicious cuisine, which varies from region to region. Food is often prepared in large quantities for festivals and celebrations and is shared among family members and guests.

Finally, Hindus also practice daily rituals as a family, such as morning prayers or the recitation of mantras. These rituals are considered a way to connect with the divine and strengthen family bonds.

Hinduism and the Calendar

In Hinduism, the calendar is an important tool for determining the dates of festivals and religious celebrations. The Hindu calendar is based on a luni-solar system, which means it uses both the movements of the Moon and the Sun to determine days, months, and years.

The Hindu calendar is very complex and varies from region to region in India. However, overall, it consists of twelve lunar months, each starting with the new moon and lasting approximately 29.5 days. These months are named after the star constellations visible in the night sky during that time. The first month is called Chaitra and corresponds to the end of winter, while the last month, Phalguna, corresponds to the end of winter.

The Hindu calendar also includes festivals and celebrations, which are often associated with mythological or historical events. The dates of these festivals are often determined based on the alignment of stars and the Moon. For example, the festival of Diwali, which marks the Hindu New Year, is celebrated on the day of the new moon in the month of

Kartik.

In addition, the Hindu calendar includes auspicious and inauspicious days, which are determined based on Vedic astrology. Auspicious days are considered favorable for starting new projects, while inauspicious days are considered unfavorable and should be avoided.

It is important to note that the Hindu calendar is intimately linked to spirituality and religion. The dates of festivals and celebrations are determined based on the alignment of stars and the Moon, but also based on the spiritual teachings of Hinduism. Thus, the Hindu calendar is an essential tool for understanding the culture and traditions of Hinduism.

Food and Eating Habits

Food and eating habits occupy an important place in the daily life of Hindus. The diet varies depending on the region in India, but certain rules are common to all Hindus.

First and foremost, food is considered sacred and must be treated with respect. Hindus follow strict rules regarding the preparation of food, the use of certain ingredients, and the timing of meals.

Food must be prepared in hygienic conditions and must be offered to God before being consumed. This offering is known as «prasad» and is believed to be blessed by the gods. The food offered as prasad is usually shared with family members and friends.

The consumption of meat is often avoided, especially by Hindus who follow vegetarianism. Cows are considered sacred and their meat is therefore forbidden. Hindus also avoid eating pork and poultry.

Spices are widely used in Indian cuisine, not only for their flavor but also for their medicinal properties. Common spices include turmeric, cumin, ginger, chili, and coriander. Hindus believe that certain spices can help heal certain ailments and improve digestion.

Meals are often vegetarian and include a variety of vegetables, grains, legumes, and dairy products. Foods are often prepared with ghee (clarified butter) and yogurt to add flavor and texture.

Meals are often accompanied by flatbread called «roti» or «chapati». Rice is also a staple food in many regions of India. Sweet desserts are also popular, such as «gulab jamun» (sugar syrup-soaked donuts) and «rasgulla» (cheese balls cooked in sugar syrup).

Furthermore, Hindus have strict rules regarding meals and food consumption. They believe that food should be eaten in a calm and peaceful atmosphere and that it should be consumed slowly and with gratitude.

Castes and Hindu Society

The caste system (varnas)

The caste system (varnas) is a major characteristic of Hindu society, which has been a source of fascination, controversy, and debate for both foreigners and locals. The varnas are the four major socio-professional categories that make up traditional Hindu society: the Brahmins, the Kshatriyas, the Vaishyas, and the Shudras. Each of these categories has a specific role in society and is associated with particular duties and responsibilities.

The Brahmins are the priests and scholars who are responsible for the preservation and interpretation of sacred texts. They are considered the highest caste due to their spiritual and intellectual role in society. The Kshatriyas are the warriors and rulers who are tasked with protecting society and maintaining order. They are also responsible for tax collection and wealth redistribution. The Vaishyas are the merchants and farmers who are in charge of production and trade. Lastly, the Shudras are the manual laborers who are responsible for the lowest and most menial tasks in society.

Although the caste system has been a feature of Hindu society for centuries, it has been criticized for its unfairness and lack of equality. The Dalits, also known as «untouchables,» are outside the caste system and are considered the lowest caste in society. They are often victims of discrimination, violence, and marginalization.

Despite this, the caste system continues to have a significant influence in Indian society. Even though discrimination is illegal, it is still practiced in many areas of life such as education, employment, and marriage. However, there have been social movements and reforms to combat caste-based injustice and discrimination.

Jatis and local communities

In Hinduism, jatis are social groups that correspond to specific professions or trades. Jatis often have unique traditions, customs, and particular religious practices that are often tied to the profession or trade of the group. For example, farmers may worship the goddess of fertility, while artisans may have rituals for their tools. Jatis are of great importance in Hindu society as they form the basis of division of labor and specialization of professions.

Hindu society is traditionally divided into four major castes (varnas): Brahmins (priests and scholars), Kshatriyas (warriors and rulers), Vaishyas (merchants and farmers), and Shudras (manual laborers and artisans). Each caste is further divided into several jatis, which are determined based on the occupational activity of its members.

Jatis hold great importance in the social and religious life of Hindus. The members of the same jati consider themselves as one large family and often share close bonds, especially during religious ceremonies, festivals, and marriages. Jatis can also be organized into local communities, which regularly gather for social and religious activities. These local communities often have a temple or shrine dedicated to their patron deity.

It is worth noting that the caste system has been widely criticized for being discriminatory and unjust towards certain castes and communities. Many social and reform movements in India have fought for the abolition of this system and equality of rights for all. Despite this, jatis continue to have a strong presence in the social and religious life of modern India.

Social Hierarchy and Power Dynamics

Social hierarchy in Hinduism is often associated with the caste system, called varnas. This system is based on birth and is considered hierarchical as it divides society into four major categories. The varnas are the Brahmins (priests), the Kshatriyas (warriors and rulers), the Vaishyas (merchants and artisans), and the Shudras (servants). While this system is often criticized for its rigidity, it has also contributed to social stability and the definition of social roles in Hindu society.

It is important to note that the caste system is not absolutely rigid and immutable. There are also subgroups of castes, called jatis, which are determined by occupation, geography, and local customs. Jatis are often further divided into sub-castes, which are also based on occupation and local traditions.

Social relations in Hindu society are often determined by caste status. People of higher caste tend to be more respected and have more opportunities, while those of lower caste are often marginalized and discriminated against. However, it is important to note that caste-based discrimination is illegal in India today, and many social movements are fighting against this practice.

In terms of power, Brahmins traditionally held the highest positions in Hindu society as priests and teachers. Kshatriyas were the rulers and warriors, while Vaishyas were traders and artisans. Shudras were often manual laborers and servants.

However, there have been reform movements that have sought to challenge this social hierarchy. For example, the Bhakti movement promoted spiritual equality and rejected social distinctions based on caste. Similarly, contemporary social movements seek to promote equality and combat caste-based discrimination.

Reforms and Anti-Caste Movements

The caste system is an important aspect of Hinduism, but it is also controversial and criticized by many Hindus and non-Hindus alike. Over the centuries, various reform movements have sought to abolish or reform the caste system, while others have sought to reinforce the existing social hierarchy.

The early reform movements began in the 19th century, under the influence of the West and ideas of freedom, equality, and justice. These movements criticized the caste system as unfair and discriminatory. They also criticized the unfair treatment of women and Dalits (the untouchables, the lowest in the social hierarchy).

One of the early reform movements was initiated by Raja Ram Mohan Roy, who founded the Brahmo Samaj in 1828. The movement called for the abolition of outdated and discriminatory practices of Hinduism, such as sati (the self-immolation of widows on their husband's funeral pyre) and idolatry.

Another significant movement was launched by Swami Dayananda Saraswati, who founded the Arya Samaj in 1875. The movement sought to return to the sacred texts of Hinduism and reject corrupt and outdated practices. It also criticized the caste system and called for equality and brotherhood among all human beings.

In the 20th century, reform movements continued, with figures such as B.R. Ambedkar, who fought for the rights of Dalits and founded the Social Justice Party in 1924. Ambedkar also played a key role in drafting India's Constitution in 1950, which banned caste-based discrimination.

However, despite these reform movements, the caste system still persists in contemporary Hindu society, and many Dalits continue to face discrimination and violence. Anti-caste movements such as the Dalit Panther and the Bhim Army have been formed to fight against this discrimination, but their influence is still limited.

Women in Hinduism

Goddesses and Female Myths

In Hinduism, goddesses hold an important place. They represent the feminine aspects of the supreme divinity, often referred to as Devi or Shakti. Hindu goddesses are revered throughout India and embody different aspects of human life, from fertility to war, love, and wisdom.

Among the most popular goddesses are Parvati, Lakshmi, and Sarasvati. Parvati, also known as Durga, is the goddess of war and the destroyer of evil forces. She is often depicted with multiple arms, each holding a different weapon. Lakshmi is the goddess of wealth, prosperity, and fortune. She is often depicted with gold coins falling from her hands. Sarasvati is the goddess of wisdom, arts, and music. She is often depicted with a musical instrument in her hands and a book by her side.

The myths and legends surrounding Hindu goddesses are numerous and diverse. For example, the legend of Parvati's birth tells that her parents, King Himavat and his wife Mena, prayed to the god Shiva to grant them a daughter. Shiva then created Parvati from his divine energy, and she became Shiva's wife after defeating many demons.

Another legend is that of Lakshmi, who appeared during the churning of the milk ocean, an important episode in Hindu mythology. The gods and demons united to churn the milk ocean in order to obtain the elixir of immortality. When

Lakshmi appeared, the gods immediately chose her as their goddess of wealth and prosperity.

Hindu goddesses have also played an important role in the daily lives of Indians. For example, during weddings, goddesses Lakshmi and Parvati are often invoked to bring prosperity, fertility, and happiness to the couple. Indian women also pray to the goddesses for the protection of their families, fertility, and the health of their husbands and children.

The Role of Women in Hindu Society

The role of women in Hindu society is a complex and nuanced subject. While there have been challenges and inequalities in the past, women have always played an important role in Hindu culture and religion.

In Hinduism, women are seen as guardians of the home and family. They are responsible for the education of children and the management of domestic tasks. However, it is important to emphasize that this does not mean that women cannot pursue other aspirations in their lives. Hinduism encourages women to follow their dharma, their duty, and to pursue their dreams and passions.

There are also many revered goddesses in Hinduism, such as Durga, Kali, and Lakshmi, who represent power, strength, and wealth. These goddesses are often invoked in rituals and ceremonies for their protection and blessings.

In Hindu society, women have also played an important role in music, dance, and the arts in general. Famous dancers like Rukmini Devi Arundale have contributed to the preservation and expansion of traditional Indian arts.

However, it is also true that women have been victims of discrimination and injustice in certain parts of Hindu society. The practice of sati, in which widows were traditionally burned on their husband's funeral pyre, was banned in India in the 19th century. Women have also been excluded from certain rituals and ceremonies, and the caste system has often limited their opportunities.

However, many women have also been important figures in the fight against these inequalities. Women like Sarojini Naidu and Indira Gandhi have been influential political leaders in India. Women like Kamaladevi Chattopadhyay and Mridula Sarabhai have worked for women's education and rights in Indian society.

Ultimately, the role of women in Hindu society is a complex subject that requires a deep understanding of culture and religion. While there have been inequalities and injustices, women have also played important roles in religion, arts, and politics. It is important to continue working towards gender equality and creating a society where women can pursue their dreams and passions without being limited by stereotypes or restrictive traditions.

Women and Religious Rituals

Women have played an important role in the religious rituals of Hinduism for centuries. Women have been involved in religious rituals since Vedic times, and their role has evolved over time. Hinduism is a religion that places great importance on family and community, and women have played a crucial role in preserving these values.

In ancient times, women were considered the guardians of the home and were responsible for performing domestic rituals. Women were often initiated into the practice of Hinduism at a young age and encouraged to continue practicing throughout their lives.

Women have also played an important role in public rituals. They have participated in processions and group religious ceremonies and sung bhajans (devotional songs). Women have also taken part in religious festivals and celebrations such as Navratri, Diwali, and Holi, wearing traditional clothes and preparing special dishes for the family and guests.

Over time, the role of women in religious rituals has evolved. Women have started to hold priestess positions and offer prayers and offerings in temples. Women have also begun to practice yoga and meditation to deepen their religious practice.

Despite these advancements, women have often been relegated to subordinate roles in religious rituals. Women have been excluded from certain temples and rituals due to their gender. However, in recent decades, women have begun to assert their place in religious rituals and demand gender equality.

Today, more and more women are involved in religious rituals and hold priestess positions in temples. Women have also started gathering in groups to discuss spirituality and Hinduism and participate in training programs to deepen their understanding of the religion.

Hinduism and Science

Cosmology and Astronomy

Cosmology and astronomy hold a significant place in Hinduism as they are closely connected to religion and philosophy. The sacred texts of Hinduism contain numerous references to astronomy, cosmology, and astrology.

The ancient Hindus were keen observers of the sky. They had noticed that the movements of celestial bodies were regular and predictable. As a result, they developed lunar and solar calendars to organize their daily lives and religious ceremonies.

Hindus believed that the universe was eternal, always existing and will always exist. They thought that the universe was composed of five elements: ether, air, fire, water, and earth. These elements are closely related to the five senses and organs of perception.

The sacred texts of Hinduism also describe the universe as a series of superimposed worlds, each inhabited by living beings. The universe is divided into four main parts: the world of the gods (Devaloka), the world of ancestors (Pitraloka), the world of living beings (Bhuloka), and the underworld (Patala).

Astronomy and astrology are also highly significant in Hinduism. Hindus believed that the movements of celestial bodies had an influence on earthly events, and they used astrology to predict the future and make important decisions.

One of the most important sacred texts of Hinduism, the Mahabharata, contains passages that describe the positions of stars and planets. The Bhagavad-Gita, another significant sacred text of Hinduism, also describes the positions of stars and planets, as well as their influence on human beings.

The ancient Hindus had extensive knowledge about celestial bodies. They knew about the existence of seven planets, including the Earth, and they understood that planets followed elliptical paths around the Sun. They also developed theories about solar and lunar eclipses.

Mathematics and the Philosophy of Numbers

Mathematics and the philosophy of numbers play a prominent role in Hinduism. Mathematics has been developed in India since antiquity, and Hinduism has greatly contributed to its advancement. Indian mathematics has had a major impact on Western science and philosophy.

The philosophy of numbers in Hinduism is based on the belief that numbers have symbolic and spiritual meanings. The number one represents unity, supreme consciousness, and the Absolute. The number two symbolizes duality, polarity, and complementarity. The number three is considered the ultimate sacred number, representing the trinity of Brahma, Vishnu, and Shiva, as well as the three gunas, or fundamental qualities of nature. Other numbers also have symbolic and spiritual meanings.

The numerical system used in Hinduism is the positional

decimal system, which was developed in India in the 3rd century BCE. This system was introduced to the West by Arabs and is now used worldwide. Additionally, Indian mathematicians developed concepts such as zero, infinity, decimal notation, and trigonometric functions.

Mathematics and the philosophy of numbers are also related to rituals and practices in Hinduism. For example, the mandala is a sacred geometric pattern used in Hindu and Buddhist rituals to represent the universe and divinity. Yantras are sacred geometric diagrams used in meditation and prayer. Mantras are sacred sound formulas repeated to attract divine energy.

Finally, mathematics and the philosophy of numbers also have practical importance in Hinduism. For instance, Hindu astrologers use mathematics to calculate horoscopes and favorable periods for celebrations and rituals. Ayurveda, traditional Indian medicine, also employs mathematics to calculate doshas, or constitutional types, and suitable treatments.

Traditional Medicine (Ayurveda)

Ayurveda, traditional Indian medicine, is one of the most fascinating aspects of Hinduism that significantly influences the health and well-being of people in India and around the world. Ayurveda is a holistic healthcare system that focuses on natural healing and disease prevention rather than symptom treatment.

Ayurveda recognizes that each individual is unique and that their health depends on various factors, including diet, lifestyle, environment, emotions, and thoughts. According to Ayurveda, maintaining a balance among the three doshas, or bodily humors, is essential for good health. The three doshas are Vata (air and ether), Pitta (fire and water), and Kapha (water and earth). Each person has a unique combination of these doshas, which determines their temperament and physical constitution.

Ayurvedic treatment is personalized based on individual and constitutional factors. It includes a combination of therapies such as herbal medicine, dietetics, massage, meditation, and yoga. Medicinal plants are extensively used in Ayurveda for their healing properties. Massages and herbal baths are also considered important means to balance doshas and restore health.

In addition to treating diseases, Ayurveda aims at disease prevention and quality of life improvement. Diet plays a crucial role in Ayurveda as it is considered a significant means to maintain dosha balance. Foods are classified according to their effects on doshas, and specific recommendations are given for each constitution type.

Ayurveda is also connected to spirituality, as it believes that physical and mental health are closely related to spiritual balance. Meditation and yoga practices are encouraged to enhance mental and emotional well-being.

Although Ayurveda has been practiced for thousands of years in India, it is gaining increasing global interest due to its holistic approach to health and well-being. However, it is important to note that Ayurveda should not be used as a substitute for conventional medical treatments for serious illnesses. It is recommended to consult a qualified Ayurvedic practitioner for personalized health assessment and advice on suitable treatments.

Ecology and Environmental Preservation

Ecology and environmental preservation are key concepts in Hinduism. This religion, founded on the belief in the divinity of nature, encourages Hindus to live in harmony with their natural environment. The sacred texts of Hinduism, such as the Vedas and the Upanishads, present nature as a manifestation of the supreme divinity and urge people to respect and protect it.

Hindu practices, such as vegetarianism and ahimsa (non-violence), reflect this approach to nature. Hindus avoid eating meat as it involves killing animals, which is considered contrary to the principles of ahimsa. Additionally, Hindus are encouraged to treat animals with respect and refrain from causing harm to them.

Yoga and meditation are also common practices in Hinduism that help develop self-awareness and a deep connection with nature. Hindus are encouraged to meditate in natural settings such as forests, mountains, or rivers to strengthen their bond with nature.

Ecology and environmental preservation are also significant

concerns for Hindu communities worldwide. Hindus have established numerous environmental advocacy groups, such as the Centre for Science and Environment (CSE) in India, which works towards promoting ecology and protecting the environment.

Ecology and environmental preservation are closely related to the concepts of dharma and karma in Hinduism. Dharma is the moral and ethical duty of every individual towards society and nature, and karma is the law of cause and effect that governs the universe. By taking care of the environment, Hindus can accumulate positive karma and contribute to the harmony of the universe.

Lastly, Hinduism also promotes the practice of organic farming, which involves cultivating food without using environmentally harmful chemicals. This practice is known as krishi sanskriti, or traditional agriculture, and is seen as a means to preserve biodiversity and protect the environment.

Hindu Art and Culture

Temple Architecture

Hindu temple architecture is an essential aspect of the religious practice of Hinduism. Temples are considered as the abodes of Hindu deities and are built to facilitate communion between the believers and the gods. Temples also serve as centers of social and cultural life, where worshipers can gather to pray, celebrate festivals, discuss spiritual matters, or simply relax.

Hindu temples come in various forms, sizes, and architectural styles, depending on the regions, eras, and local traditions. However, all temples have common architectural elements that are determined by the fundamental principles of Hindu cosmology and symbolism.

Most temples are built according to a square or rectangular plan, divided into several sections, each with its own symbolic meaning. The outer courtyard, or mandapa, is often used for gatherings and celebrations, while the main hall, or garbhagriha, houses the statue or representation of the deity. The garbhagriha is located at the center of the temple and is considered the focal point of the structure. The walls and ceilings of temples are richly adorned with sculptures, paintings, and engravings, depicting scenes from Hindu mythology or sacred symbols.

Hindu temples are often constructed with stone, marble, or granite, but some are also built with wood, clay, or bricks.

The older temples often feature simple geometric patterns, while newer temples are more elaborate and decorated with intricate sculptures and complex engravings.

An important element of temple architecture is the gopuram, or monumental entrance tower, which is often adorned with sculptures and colorful motifs. The gopuram is usually located at the entrance of the temple and marks the sacred entrance. Visitors often have to pass through multiple successive gates to reach the main sanctuary.

Sculpture and Painting

Sculpture and painting are key elements of Hindu art and culture. For centuries, art has been used to tell stories, express emotions, and pay tribute to Hindu deities. Sculptures and paintings often depict mythological or religious scenes, but they can also represent historical characters or events from daily life.

Sculptures are often made of stone, bronze, wood, or terracotta. Stone sculptures are particularly famous for their beauty and intricacy. Hindu temples are adorned with magnificent sculptures that often depict Hindu deities in different poses and manifestations. Bronze sculptures are also very popular and are often used as objects of worship in homes and temples.

Paintings, on the other hand, are often created on canvases or temple walls. Hindu mural paintings are particularly famous for their beauty and richness. They often depict mythological scenes or episodes from the lives of Hindu deities. Canvas paintings are also very popular and are often used for home decoration.

An interesting aspect of Hindu art and culture is the use of symbols and motifs. Symbols such as the lotus, swastika, and Om are ubiquitous in Hindu art. They are often used to represent Hindu deities or symbolize key concepts such as creation, reincarnation, and spiritual awakening. Motifs such as mandalas and yantras are also very common and are often used for meditation and contemplation.

Classical Indian Dance and Music

Dance and classical music are important aspects of Hindu culture. Indian dance, also known as «Natya Shastra,» is a form of artistic expression that combines body movements, facial expressions, and hand gestures to tell stories and represent emotions. Classical Indian music, on the other hand, is characterized by complex melodies and rhythms.

The origin of Indian dance dates back thousands of years. It is often associated with deities and is used in religious rituals to honor the gods and goddesses. There are many different classical Indian dances, but the most well-known ones are Bharatanatyam, Kathak, Manipuri, Kuchipudi, Odissi, and Mohiniattam. Each dance style has its own distinct movements, costumes, and styles of music.

Classical Indian music is divided into two main categories: North Indian music, called Hindustani, and South Indian music, called Carnatic. Both styles are based on a system of ragas, which are complex and modulated melodies that evoke specific emotional effects. Indian musicians also use talas, which are rhythmic cycles.

Indian dance and classical music have been influenced by the different cultures and religions that have passed through India over the centuries. The traditions of Indian dance and music have also been passed down from generation to generation, from guru to disciple.

Today, Indian dance and classical music are appreciated worldwide. Indian dance and classical music festivals attract artists and audiences from around the world. Many Indian dancers and musicians have also achieved international fame.

Cinema and Hinduism

Indian cinema is one of the largest contributors to global cinema, producing more films than any other country. It is therefore natural that Hinduism has a significant presence in the Indian film industry.

Indian cinema, often referred to as «Bollywood,» is famous for its dance and music scenes, which are often inspired by Hindu culture and religion. Bollywood films often have a religious dimension, with scenes of worship, rituals, and prayers.

Hinduism is also represented in the scripts of many

Indian films, which often explore themes such as karma, reincarnation, devotion, and spirituality. Some of the most popular films in India, such as «Lagaan» and «PK,» have creatively and innovatively addressed religious and philosophical themes.

Indian cinema has also had an impact on Hinduism itself, popularizing religious practices among the general public. For example, meditation and yoga are becoming increasingly popular in India and around the world, thanks to their positive portrayal in Bollywood films.

Outside of India, Hinduism has also inspired many foreign filmmakers. Films such as «Samsara» by Ron Fricke and «Baraka» by Mark Magidson, which explore themes of spirituality and religion, have been influenced by ideas and concepts from Hinduism.

Literature and Poetry

Literature and poetry are fundamental elements of Hindu culture and play an important role in the religion of Hinduism. The sacred texts of Hinduism, such as the Vedas, Upanishads, Mahabharata, Bhagavad-Gita, and Ramayana, are rich in poetry and prose and constitute a literary treasure for Hindus and non-Hindus alike.

The Vedas are the oldest texts of Hinduism and are considered the foundations of Hindu culture and religion. They are written in Sanskrit and include hymns and prayers to various Hindu deities. The Upanishads, which were written at a later period, are a series of philosophical texts that explore concepts such as Brahman, Atman, karma, reincarnation, and moksha.

The Mahabharata is an epic poem that tells the story of the Kuru dynasty and the war between the Kauravas and the Pandavas. The Bhagavad-Gita is a part of the Mahabharata and contains Krishna's teachings to Prince Arjuna on dharma, karma, and reincarnation. The Ramayana is another epic poem that narrates the story of Prince Rama and his wife Sita.

The Puranas are a collection of texts that narrate the stories of Hindu gods and goddesses and their avatars. They are written in a narrative and poetic style and are often accompanied by philosophical commentaries.

The Tantra texts, which were written at a later period, are a series of esoteric texts that explore spiritual and sexual practices of tantra.

Hindu poetry and literature are also rich in regional diversity. Regional languages such as Tamil, Telugu, Kannada, and Bengali have their own distinct literature and poetry, often associated with regional religious movements such as Shaivism and Vaishnavism.

The art of poetry is also practiced in the religious practices of Hinduism, particularly in devotional songs such as bhajans and kirtans, which are sung in honor of Hindu deities. Bhajans are often accompanied by traditional musical instruments such as the tabla, harmonium, and sitar, and are sung in groups during religious celebrations and festivals.

Hinduism and other religions

Interactions with Buddhism and Jainism

In the history of India, Buddhism and Jainism have played a significant role in the formation of Hinduism. Although the two religions have notable differences from Hinduism, they have influenced Hindu philosophy and spirituality. In this section, we will examine the historical interactions between Hinduism, Buddhism, and Jainism.

Buddhism was founded by Siddhartha Gautama in the 6th century BCE. As a prince, he left the comfort of his palace to discover the truth of life and ultimately reached enlightenment under a Bodhi tree. Buddhism is based on the Four Noble Truths and the Noble Eightfold Path. Buddhism focuses on the cessation of suffering and the pursuit of enlightenment. The Buddha's doctrine rejects deities, caste, reincarnation, and the existence of a permanent self.

Buddhism has influenced Hinduism in several ways. Firstly, Buddhist ideas led to the emergence of the philosophical school of Madhyamaka, which had a great influence on the development of Vedanta, a school of Hindu philosophy. Additionally, the notion of illusion (maya) in Hinduism has been influenced by Buddhist philosophy. Moreover, certain texts such as the Mahabharata and the Bhagavad-Gita present Buddhist ideas such as non-violence, equality of all creatures, and the need to transcend desire.

Jainism is an Indian religion that was founded in the 6th

century BCE. Jainism was founded by Mahavira, who was a contemporary of the Buddha. Jainism is based on beliefs in non-violence (ahimsa), truth (satya), non-stealing (asteya), chastity (brahmacharya), and non-attachment (aparigraha). Jainism advocates for the liberation of the individual soul (jiva) from the cycle of reincarnation (samsara) and its union with the divine (moksha).

Jainism has influenced Hinduism in multiple ways. Firstly, the concept of non-violence (ahimsa) is common to both religions. Additionally, the practice of meditation and the pursuit of liberation of the soul are also shared. Finally, Jain texts have influenced Hindu texts such as the Puranas.

Relations with Islam and Sikhism

The relations between Hinduism, Islam, and Sikhism are complex and often tumultuous. India has experienced many periods of tension between these three religions, but it has also seen periods of peaceful coexistence and religious syncretism.

Islam was introduced to India in the 7th century by Arab and Persian traders, but it wasn't until the 12th century that Muslims began to establish a lasting presence in the country, with the invasion of the Punjab region by Muslim troops. Over the following centuries, the relations between Hindus and Muslims were marked by conflicts, persecutions, and massacres, particularly during the Mughal Empire, which ruled over India from the 16th to the 19th century.

Sikhism, on the other hand, emerged in response to Muslim dominance in the Punjab region in the 16th century. The founder of Sikhism, Guru Nanak, advocated for a religion based on tolerance, equality, and social justice. Sikhs fought against Muslims to defend their religion and territory, but they also worked with them to promote peace and coexistence.

Despite past conflicts, there is today a significant Muslim community in India, representing about 14% of the population. Indian Muslims have their own customs and traditions, but they have also adopted elements of Hindu and Indian culture.

Similarly, Sikhs and Hindus have significant religious and cultural differences, but they also have a long history of cooperation and mutual tolerance. Hindus and Sikhs have worked together to resist attempts of Muslim domination, and they have also collaborated to promote peace and prosperity in Indian society.

Influences on and from Western religions

The influence of Hinduism on Western religions dates back several centuries. During the Middle Ages, Arab merchants introduced Hindu mathematical and astronomical knowledge to Europe, which influenced the Renaissance and modern science. However, the influence of Hinduism on Western religions is more complex and subtle than a simple transmission of knowledge.

One of the most evident examples of Hinduism's influence

on Western religions is the growing popularity of yoga and meditation. These practices were introduced to the West by Hindu spiritual masters such as Swami Vivekananda and Paramahansa Yogananda in the early 20th century. Since then, they have become common practices in many Western religions and spiritual disciplines, including Buddhism, Christianity, and even the business world.

Furthermore, the Western understanding of spirituality and religion has been influenced by Hindu concepts of karma, reincarnation, and liberation. Western philosophers and writers, such as Ralph Waldo Emerson and Henry David Thoreau, have been inspired by the teachings of the Bhagavad-Gita and the Upanishads.

The influence of Hinduism on Western culture can also be observed in art and music. Western artists and musicians have been influenced by the rhythms and melodies of Hindu music, as well as the artistic representations of Hindu gods and goddesses.

Conversely, Western religions have also influenced Hinduism. Christian missionaries introduced the idea of a singular God, which influenced Hindu concepts of divinity such as Ishvara. Additionally, Hinduism has been influenced by Islam, Buddhism, and Jainism, all of which have left their mark on Hindu religion and culture.

Hinduism Today

The Practice of Hinduism Worldwide

The practice of Hinduism is widespread around the world and is followed by millions of people, primarily in India but also in other regions across the globe. Religious practices vary based on different schools and individual beliefs of followers, but there are common practices among all Hindus.

Hindu religious practices include rituals and ceremonies that can be performed in temples or at home. Pujas, or religious celebrations, are often conducted daily and involve offerings to Hindu gods and goddesses. Practitioners may offer flowers, food, and prayers during these ceremonies.

In addition to pujas, Hinduism practitioners may also participate in festivals and religious celebrations throughout the year. These festivals include Diwali, the festival of lights, Holi, the festival of colors, and Navratri, the festival of nine nights.

Yoga and meditation are also significant practices in Hinduism. Yoga is a physical and mental practice that aims to unite the body and mind. It is often associated with meditation and relaxation and is used to enhance the spirituality and mental well-being of practitioners.

Ahimsa, or non-violence, is an important practice in Hinduism. This practice involves respect and compassion for all living beings, including animals and plants. Hindus may choose to be vegetarian or vegan due to this belief in ahimsa.

Pilgrimages are also a common practice in Hinduism. Practitioners may visit holy places such as sacred rivers, mountains, and temples to deepen their spirituality and connection to their religious beliefs.

Outside of India, Hinduism is also practiced in other regions of the world, including Southeast Asia, East Africa, North America, and Europe. Hindu communities in these regions may follow unique forms of Hinduism that reflect local cultures and beliefs.

Contemporary Issues and Challenges

In the contemporary world, Hinduism faces several issues and challenges that significantly impact its practice and perception worldwide. One of the most significant issues is the preservation of Hindu traditions and culture in the face of globalization and modernization. With the dissemination of information worldwide, cultural boundaries are becoming increasingly blurred, and traditional Hindu values are often questioned. It is crucial for Hindus to strike a balance between modernity and tradition and preserve their culture and values in an ever-changing world.

Another major challenge is the relationship between Hinduism and other religions. While Hinduism has a long history of peaceful interactions and dialogue with other religions, it also faces religious conflicts, particularly with Islam and Christianity. Religious tensions can be exacerbated by political, economic, and social issues and can lead to religious violence and discrimination. It is essential for Hindus to continue promoting interreligious dialogue and peaceful coexistence while defending their own religious beliefs and practices.

Hinduism also faces internal challenges, particularly regarding the representation and participation of women. Despite having a rich and complex tradition concerning the role of women, they are often underrepresented in religious practices and rituals. It is important for Hindus to address this situation by giving greater visibility and participation to women in religious and cultural life.

Another significant challenge is the preservation of the environment and ecology. Hinduism has a long tradition of respect and reverence for nature, but this tradition is often threatened by economic growth and environmental degradation. It is essential for Hindus to reaffirm their commitment to environmental protection and promote sustainable and nature-friendly practices.

Lastly, Hinduism faces challenges regarding the education and training of the younger generations. As the world rapidly changes, it is important for Hindus to pass on the values and traditions of Hinduism to the younger generations. This can be achieved through formal and informal education, as well as active participation of the youth in religious and cultural practices.

Hinduism and Science

Hinduism is a complex religion that encompasses a multitude of beliefs and practices, including scientific aspects. The scientific approach in Hinduism is often different from that of other religions, as it is based on empirical methods and concrete observations rather than blind faith.

Astronomy is one of the most developed scientific fields in Hinduism. Ancient sacred texts such as the Vedas and Puranas contain detailed information about astronomy and cosmology, including precise calculations of star and planetary positions. For example, the Aryabhatiya, a mathematical treatise written by Indian astronomer Aryabhata in the 5th century, provides intricate details about the solar system and the movement of celestial bodies with great accuracy.

Similarly, traditional Indian medicine, known as Ayurveda, is based on a holistic approach that treats the body, mind, and soul as interconnected entities. Ayurveda practitioners use herbs, spices, and other natural remedies to treat a variety of illnesses, focusing on prevention rather than symptom treatment. This approach is increasingly recognized in Western countries as an effective alternative to modern medical treatments.

Hinduism also regards the natural environment as sacred and advocates for its preservation. This vision is put into practice through ecological practices such as recycling, the use of renewable energy sources, and the protection of endangered species.

Hinduism and Ecology

Hinduism is a complex religion that advocates for a deep understanding of the relationship between humans and nature. Ecology is therefore a central concept in this religion. The teachings of Hinduism show us that everything in the universe is interconnected, and the protection of the environment is a moral duty.

Hinduism teaches that nature is sacred and that we must protect it. This protection is particularly important today as the environment is threatened by overconsumption, pollution, and climate change. Hindus have a particular responsibility towards nature because they consider it divine and believe it deserves our respect and protection.

In Hinduism, the relationship between humans and nature is compared to that between a mother and her child. Just as a child relies on its mother for survival, humans depend on nature for sustenance. Nature is our nurturing mother, providing everything we need to live. Therefore, we have a duty to protect and preserve it.

Hinduism encourages the practice of ahimsa or non-violence towards all living beings. Hindus are encouraged not to harm animals or nature in general. This often translates into vegetarianism, which is a common practice among Hindus. This practice helps protect animals and reduces the environmental impact of the meat industry.

Yoga and meditation, two common practices in Hinduism, also encourage a connection with nature. By meditating outdoors or practicing yoga in nature, Hindus can connect with the environment and become aware of the significance of nature in their lives.

Hinduism also advocates for the preservation of biodiversity and ecosystems. Hindus are encouraged to preserve forests, rivers, and oceans as well as the fauna and flora living in them. The protection of endangered species is also promoted.

Hinduism also encourages the practice of voluntary simplicity, which involves living with less and reducing consumption to lessen one's impact on the environment. Hindus are encouraged not to be attached to material possessions and not to seek the accumulation of material wealth.

In conclusion, Hinduism is a religion that advocates for environmental protection and connection with nature. The teachings of this religion can serve as an inspiration for those seeking to protect the environment and reduce their impact on nature. Hindus have a moral duty towards nature and must continue to promote environmental protection for future generations.

Conclusion

The richness and diversity of Hinduism

Hinduism is a rich and diverse religion that offers a multitude of perspectives and practices. Indeed, while there are common characteristics among all Hindu currents and schools of thought, Hinduism is a complex, pluralistic, and evolving universe.

The richness of Hinduism lies in the diversity of its practices and beliefs. For example, while some schools of thought emphasize the importance of devotion and service to the gods, others focus on asceticism and meditation. Furthermore, while some Hindu practices are reserved for priests and initiates, others are open to all believers.

Hinduism is also a religion that has adapted and transformed over time. Hindu practices and beliefs have been influenced by contacts with other cultures such as the Persians, Greeks, Arabs, and Europeans. Similarly, Hinduism has also influenced other religions such as Buddhism and Jainism.

The diversity of Hinduism is also reflected in its various branches and schools of thought. Vedicism, for example, is an ancient branch of Hinduism that focuses on sacrifices and rituals. Shaivism, on the other hand, emphasizes devotion to the god Shiva, while Vaishnavism focuses on the god Vishnu. Shaktism, in turn, emphasizes devotion to the mother goddess, Shakti.

Hinduism also offers a rich variety of sacred texts, each with its own history and meaning. The Vedas are the oldest and most important texts in Hinduism, while the Bhagavad-Gita is one of the most popular and widely studied texts worldwide. The Puranas and Tantric texts, on the other hand, explore the mythological and esoteric aspects of Hinduism.

Finally, the richness of Hinduism is also reflected in its art and culture. The architecture of temples, Hindu sculptures, and paintings are famous worldwide for their beauty and refinement. Similarly, Indian classical dance and music have a long history and great cultural significance.

The importance of Hinduism in the modern world

Hinduism is one of the oldest and most influential religions in the world, and its importance cannot be underestimated. With over a billion practitioners worldwide, Hinduism is the third most practiced religion after Christianity and Islam.

In addition to being a religion, Hinduism is a way of life, a philosophy, and a culture. The importance of Hinduism in the modern world lies in its ability to adapt and transform while preserving its traditions and fundamental values. The teachings of Hinduism, such as Dharma, Karma, and reincarnation, have been integrated into the thinking and culture of many societies, influencing the world in many areas.

Hinduism also has great importance in the world of spirituality. The practices of yoga and meditation, which were developed in Hinduism, have become popular worldwide. These practices are recognized for their benefits to mental and physical health and are increasingly used in modern medical treatments.

Furthermore, Hinduism has had a significant influence on culture and the arts. Indian classical dances and music are closely related to Hindu religion. Epic poems such as the Mahabharata and the Ramayana have been a source of inspiration for writers and filmmakers around the world. The richness of Hindu art and culture is evidence of the importance of Hinduism in the modern world.

Hinduism has also been a catalyst for social change. Reforms initiated by personalities like Raja Ram Mohan Roy and Mahatma Gandhi have led to the abolition of unjust social practices such as the caste system and discrimination against women. Hinduism has also been a driving force behind the independence movement in India, which ultimately led to the liberation of the country from colonial rule.

Finally, Hinduism has great importance in today's world regarding the preservation of the environment and ecology. The teachings of Hinduism emphasize respect for nature and harmony with the environment. Many Hindus have adopted ecological lifestyles by using renewable energy, protecting animals, and reducing their meat consumption.

Acknowledgment

Dear readers,

Firstly, I would like to express my sincerest gratitude for taking the time to delve into the fascinating world of Hinduism. Your curiosity and open-mindedness are essential elements in approaching such a cultural and spiritual wealth. Through these pages, we have embarked together on a journey filled with discoveries and reflections about this ancient religion.

Like a river with multiple tributaries, Hinduism is full of currents of thought, traditions, and varied practices. It is akin to a kaleidoscope, where each facet reflects a unique dimension of this cultural and spiritual mosaic. I hope this book has awakened in you an interest and passion for the treasures that this ancient tradition holds.

It is important to emphasize that this work would not have been possible without the hard work and contributions of many researchers, scholars, writers, and artists who, over the centuries, have shed light on and shared knowledge about Hinduism. The richness of their contributions and the diversity of their viewpoints have served as the foundation for our understanding of this complex and captivating religion.

In this spirit, I invite you to continue your exploration of Hinduism beyond these pages. Do not hesitate to immerse yourself in the sacred texts, works of art, and cultural experiences to deepen and enrich your understanding of this tradition. Like a tree with deep roots, Hinduism is an inexhaustible subject that yearns to be explored.

Lastly, I sincerely thank you for your commitment to discovering Hinduism. Your interest in this religion speaks of an open and curious mind, eager to learn and understand the world around us. May this book have illuminated your path and offered you a glimpse of the beauty and complexity of Hinduism.

With all my gratitude and admiration for your quest for knowledge.

Printed in Great Britain
by Amazon

36688643R00056